Path to Prosperity

Making Vision, Mission and Objectives to Accomplish Business Greatness

James V. Brigham

Copyright:

All rights reserved. No part of this publication may be reproduced, distributed or transmitted in any form or by any means, including photocopying, recording, or other electronic or mechanical methods, without the prior written permission of the publisher, except in the case of brief quotations embodied in critical reviews and certain other non-commercial users permitted by the copyright law.

Copyright © (James V. Brigham), (2024).

Disclaimer:

The information contained in this book is for educational and informational purposes only. The content is based on the author's personal research, experiences, and opinions. While every effort has been made to ensure the accuracy and reliability of the information provided, the author and publisher assume no responsibility for errors, omissions, or any consequences arising from the use of the information in this book.

CONTENT

INTRODUCTION: 3
    YOU CAN ACHIEVE ANYTHING YOU WANT 3

CHAPTER 1 9
    UNDERSTAND THE MEANING OF VISION AND MISSION STATEMENTS IN ACHIEVING BUSINESS SIGNIFICANCE 9

CHAPTER 2 39
    WHY OBJECTIVE SETTING IS SIGNIFICANT? 39

CHAPTER 3 57
    MARGIN THE VISION, MISSION AND OBJECTIVES 57

CHAPTER 4 108
    MONETARY ADMINISTRATION FOR PROGRESS.. 109

CONCLUSION 135
    ACHIEVING BUSINESS SUCCESS 136

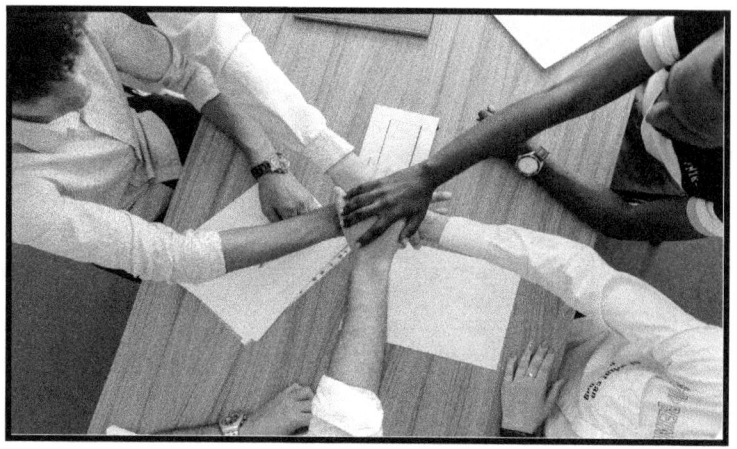

INTRODUCTION:

YOU CAN ACHIEVE ANYTHING YOU WANT

In the high-stepper field of business, where challenge is irate and the scene is never-ending moving, accomplishment relies upon some different option from troublesome work and good karma. It requires a sensible aide, a persuading reason, and a persisting drive for significance. Welcome to the **"Path to Prosperity"** by

James *V. Brigham,* your principal manual for changing craving into achievement and vision into win.

Imagine a reality where your business squeezes by as well as twists, dependably beating competitors and outperforming suspicions. A reality where your gathering is enabled, your clients are committed, and your improvement bearing is limitless. This is positively not a distant dream yet an undeniable reality, reachable through the fundamental predominance of vision, mission, and targets.

In this significant book, James V. Brigham shares his wealth of inclusion and significant encounters into the middle guidelines that help each viable business. Whether you're a financial specialist leaving on another undertaking, a painstakingly pre-approved pioneer controlling a spread out huge business, or a manager making a pass at max activity, this book will outfit you with the gadgets and strategies expected to make an undeniable vision, portray a persuading mission, and set forth imperative goals that drive upheld significance.

You will find:

The best strategy to make sense of a fantasy that is both moving and critical: Your vision fills in as the coordinating star for your business, impelling your gathering towards an ordinary objective and granting an internal compass and bearing. Brigham isolates the most widely recognized approach to making a fantasy that isn't simply hopeful yet what's more grounded really, ensuring that it might be effectively conveyed and embraced by all people from your affiliation.

The specialty of saying something of direction that embodies your business' inspiration and fundamental convictions: A solid mission statement resounds significantly with laborers, clients, and accomplices the equivalent. It portrays what your personality is, a major inspiration for you, and why you exist. Sort out some way to say something of direction that perceives your business in the business place and fills in as a stimulating wail for your gathering.

Exhibited methodologies for spreading out Wise goals (Express, Quantifiable, Reachable, Significant, Time-bound): Targets are the design blocks of business accomplishment. Brigham gives an organized construction to characterizing and achieving goals that drive execution, develop liability, and assurance predictable progression. Through practical exercises and authentic models, you will sort out some way to isolate forceful objectives into sensible, significant stages.

However, achieving business significance connects past portraying vision, mission, and targets. It incorporates fostering a culture of progression, strength, and relentless improvement. Brigham dives into the intricacies of drive, examining how visionary trailblazers can move their gatherings, investigate hardships, and change their relationship to sweeping fundamental targets and moral characteristics.

With a wealth of genuine models and logical examinations from an alternate show of adventures, this book offers utilitarian encounters into how compelling associations have investigated catches and made the most of possibilities. Each segment is planned to be both persuasive and huge, giving you the data and sureness to execute these norms in your own business setting.

As you set out on this pivotal journey, review that the mission for business significance is a significant distance race, not a run. It demands relentlessness, adaptability, and a vow to advancing learning and improvement. "Way To Success" by James V. Brigham is your trusted companion on this journey, offering the knowledge, techniques, and relief you truly need to change your vision into a prospering reality.

Oblige us in opening the way to enduring through progress. Your approach to prospering beginnings here.

CHAPTER 1

UNDERSTAND THE MEANING OF VISION AND MISSION STATEMENTS IN ACHIEVING BUSINESS SIGNIFICANCE

Whether you are operating a large design, having an association thing and vision might help to inspire attendees. The charge and vision of an association are critical to its strategy since they're employed to depict unborn pretensions and practical procedures. While the terms charge and vision are constantly used interchangeably, they actually relate to two distinct aspects of the association.

Sorting Out charge Statements

The corporation's charge statement addresses the association's business, its intentions, and its strategy for achieving those pretensions. It focuses more on where the association is right now and the critical advancements it needs to make to attain its pretensions. An association's charge statement can be employed to shape its life.

While creating a charge statement for your association, outline what your company does, who you serve, and how you serve them. These are the three most important factors of a business' charge statement. For illustration,

Amazon's charge statement reads," We try to offer our guests the most negligible likely charges, the stylish that anybody could anticipate to see as a decision, and the most elevated position of solace." awaiting an independent adventure to vend awful children's vesture, for illustration" We offer unpracticed guardians stupendous papers of apparel for their babies that are handwrought with love." This consolidates what the company does, who their target followership is, and how they serve them. It provides agents with a clear thing.

Understanding Vision Verbalizations

While the charge statement focuses on more important aspects of the establishment, the vision vocalization prepares for the association. The vision explanation outlines where the association needs to go. Along with the charge statement, it aids in the development of a defined business system.

While creating a fantasy vision for your company, respond to questions about your deepest solicitations. What kind of future do you fantasize, and how does the association play a part in driving it forward? Is it true that you want to have an impact in some way, and how should you go about it? Amazon's vision statement is" to be the world's most customer- driven association, where guests can find anything they might need to buy on the internet." It provides agents with an egregious route of action.

A dream explanation for the nonpublic bid that makes excellent child pieces of apparel could be" to be the most ideal choice for inexperienced guardians wanting to prepare their invigorated children, in particular hand customized dress that's organized and made with the best conceivable degree of responsibility." It easily illustrates where the association has to go from then on out and how it intends to achieve that status. It also contains their main selling point.

Enforcing Mission and Vision Explanations in Your Definitive system

An association's charge and vision statements aid in the design of the colorful situations of the frame. Both give provocation and pretensions, which are necessary factors of a fashion. They define the business group and what that group deems to be significant. By understanding these factors, commercial leaders may encourage a further step- by- step frame that assists the association in reaching its primary goal in a short period of time, as well as its vision in the long run.

Mission and vision statements help associations in setting prosecution guidelines and estimates grounded on the pretensions they need to attain. They also give delegates with a defined thing to achieve, enhancing viability and proficiency.

Mission and vision statements are important not only for workers and business possessors while developing a believable strategy. They also apply to external mates similar as guests, accessories, and suppliers. The thing and vision explanations can be employed as a marketing tool to draw media allowed, attract unequivocal group areas, and grow company hookups with relative associations.

Isolating between Vision and Mission

One of the critical contrasts between a dream and statement of purpose is the schedule. Vision proclamations are forward- looking. They look a long time into the future and imagine what the association needs to make. Also again, a statement of purpose is about the present. It checks out at the present status of the business, not what is to come. The vision depicts the" why" of the business, as per BetterHelp. It's the explanation that the business exists. The charge, also again, depicts the" how" of the business. It's further strategic and procedural than conclusive.

Authentic Vision and Statement of purpose Models

While allowing your business vision and statement of purpose, check out models from driving associations. Surveying fruitful business vision and statements of purpose can help you with creating them for your own association. Note how the vision proclamations are uplifting and give an illustration of what the association solicitations to come from then on out. The statements of purpose talk about what the association does at the moment and individualities they help.

The Connection Between the Plan of action and System

Many businesses require conservative intending to expand the odds of coming out on top. multitudinous private gambles can not produce gain and bomb inside the original not numerous long ages of exertion. The expressions" business system" and" plan of action" depict affiliated ideas that are vital to the cycles of arranging and dealing with a business.

Business Procedure

The expression" business methodology" depicts the ways a business utilizes to negotiate its central thing and targets. A business' main thing incorporates its general reason, abecedarian beliefs and long haul objects. A supermarket could have the charge of creating gain while giving the stylish food to guests, limiting its effect on the climate and advancing strength in the neighborhood frugality. The association's fashion could include:

Copping particularly from near food makers, empowering guests to bring their own chief sacks, publicizing in neighborhood papers and copping reused point speeding accouterments . A business' fashion incorporates the way that it manages the implicit open doors and troubles it faces.

Plan of action

An association's plan of action depicts the abecedarian means by which it makes regard, conveys worth to purchasers and gathers income from guests to produce a gain. Plans of action can change extraordinarily starting with one association also onto the coming. A neighborhood supermarket's plan of action could include copping
food at reduction costs and offering it to end guests at a more extravagant cost to produce gain. A point could have a plan of action in view of giving videotape content to guests and producing income through elevations put on the point.

How They Are Connected

An association's plan of action is a piece of its business' general procedure. It's the slapdash piece behind how the association intends to negotiate its objectives, like creating a gain. An association can change its plan of action over the long run as a piece of its benefit making procedure. For case, in the event that point does not make sufficient income from commercials to produce gain, chiefs could conclude to execute another plan of action, for illustration, dealing Shirts and different products still a web- grounded store, as a procedure to support benefit.

Field-Tested Strategy

Deciding an organization's central goal, targets, system and plan of action are extremely significant stages during the time spent making new business and can assist supervisors with framing a field-tested strategy. A strategy is a record that goes about as a diagram for how the strategies work and accomplish productivity.

Instructions to Determine an Intelligent System

You have two options in the activity of your business: assume command over your organization's course, or respond to powers outside of your reach and desire to arrive on your feet. Obviously, taking control is the better decision, and the method for doing it is by determining an intelligible system. Procedure is the piece of the business arranging process that frames the means you really want to take to contend in your market actually. It starts with an engaged assertion of your organization's motivation and passes on you prepared to execute a plainly characterized game plan to arrive at your business objectives.

1. Make a statement of purpose that characterizes your center business in a sentence or two. For instance, Amazon's statement of purpose "is to be earth's most client driven organization; to construct where individuals can come to find and find whatever they could need to purchase on the web."

2. Characterize your targets. List concrete, quantifiable objectives for the organization. Instances of objectives incorporate a particular income target or catch of a particular portion of the overall industry.

3. Direct a SWOT examination. At the end of the day, survey your organization's inward assets and shortcomings and its outside valuable open doors and dangers. Consider such inside factors as a portion of the overall industry, protected innovation, monetary assets and staff. Incorporate such outer variables as your client base, contest, merchants, financial circumstances and arising innovation.

4. Apply the bits of knowledge you gain through the SWOT investigation to recognize those that will help or obstruct your capacity to accomplish your goals.

5. Come up with your system. Characterize the particular moves you want to make to accomplish your goals. Note the means important to conquer dangers and provokes and use qualities and open doors for your potential benefit.

6. Conclude which job such partners as workers and merchants will play in the procedure. Impart these jobs plainly to welcome everybody ready. Make the procedure part of your organization's way of life

Making a Strong Vision Explanation

A strong vision proclamation is a foundation of key preparation, epitomizing the yearnings and long haul goals of an association. It fills in as a directing star, spurring and adjusting all partners towards a shared objective. Here is a bit by bit manual for making a successful vision proclamation:

1. Comprehend Your Basic beliefs and Reason

Prior to creating a dream explanation, it's critical to profoundly comprehend the association's guiding principle and reason. This includes contemplation and conversation about what genuinely drives the association and a big motivator for it. Guiding principles give the establishment whereupon the vision is fabricated, guaranteeing that it resounds legitimately with the organization's character.

2. Imagine What's in store

A dream proclamation ought to illustrate the future the association tries to make. It would be ideal for it to be forward-looking, mirroring the drawn out objectives and aspirations. Consider where you see the association in 5, 10, or even 20 years. This vision ought to be both optimistic and feasible, pushing the association to take a stab at greatness while remaining grounded truly.

3. Connect with Partners

Creating a dream explanation is certainly not a singular undertaking. Connecting with key partners, including workers, initiative, clients, and accomplices, guarantees that the vision is far reaching and comprehensive. Cooperative conversations can bring different viewpoints and thoughts, enhancing the vision and encouraging a feeling of responsibility among all included.

4. Be Clear and Succinct

A strong vision proclamation is clear, compact, and straightforward. It ought to have the option to be conveyed rapidly and recalled without any problem. Keep away from language and complex language; all things being equal, utilize basic, effective words that convey the pith of the vision. Hold back nothing that can be communicated in one to two sentences.

5. Move and Inspire

The vision articulation ought to move and rouse. It ought to bring out a feeling of fervor and responsibility, convincing individuals to pursue the imagined future. Utilize dynamic and positive language that catches the creative mind and drives excitement. The objective is to make a dream that empowers and draws in everybody inside the association.

6. Reflect Authoritative Qualities and Open doors

Think about the association's assets and the amazing open doors accessible on the lookout. The vision ought to use these qualities and line up with market patterns and open doors. This essential arrangement guarantees that the vision isn't just optimistic yet additionally reachable, grounded in the association's abilities and the outside climate.

7. Audit and Refine

Making a dream explanation is an iterative cycle. Draft numerous renditions and look for input from different partners. Refine the assertion in light of this criticism, guaranteeing that it precisely catches the association's yearnings and reverberates with all partners. A very much created vision proclamation frequently goes through a few modifications before it is concluded.

8. Convey and Implant the Vision

When the vision articulation is finished, it should be imparted really all through the association. Guarantee that each representative gets it and embraces the vision. Install the vision into the authoritative culture, integrating it into key preparation, independent direction, and day to day activities. Routinely return to and reaffirm the vision to keep it alive and pertinent.

Instances of Strong Vision Articulations:

Microsoft: "To enable each individual and each association in the world to accomplish more."

Tesla: "To make the most convincing vehicle organization of the 21st hundred years by driving the world's progress to electric vehicles."

Oxfam: "An only world without neediness."

Characterizing the Mission Explanation:

A statement of purpose, is a short, expansive assertion about an association's objectives and the way that it means to meet those objectives. It frequently addresses what the association offers and how it desires to serve its clients, local area, workers, financial backers or different partners. Some statements of purpose may likewise incorporate clarifications of the rules that the association values and desires to keep all through its presence.

An authoritative mission additionally assists with directing the activities of an association. A related however unique hierarchical assertion is the vision proclamation, a statement of what the association desires to turn into. The distinction between a mission and a dream is that the previous addresses the association's motivation, while the last option centers around goals for what was to come in light of its ongoing reason.

Hierarchical Mission

For What Reason is a Hierarchical Mission Significant?

A hierarchical mission is an assertion coordinated both inside and remotely, so it illuminates how partners at all levels see the association. Among the elements that an authoritative mission can influence are:

Brand: Brand alludes to how clients connect with an association. Part of the capability of a hierarchical mission is to decide partners, including clients, so it can act as a solicitation to the ideal interest group to investigate what the association offers. The brand likewise recognizes the association from contenders. There might be likenesses in the items or administrations that different associations sell, yet the mission can lay out a remarkable reason that resounds with clients.

Culture: Authoritative culture alludes to the work space according to an association's expressed qualities and objectives. Culture can impact how individuals from an association collaborate and work inside its framework, as it normally includes how the association treats its partners and the way in which data moves through the association. The variables that decide culture, like hierarchical qualities and standards, come from the mission.

Resolve: The authoritative mission can likewise influence how representatives connect with their obligations by conveying reason in the work they do. The mission can show that their obligations and activities are important for a bigger desire and assist them with seeing the worth in their commitments are significant. At the point when representatives see they serve a significant reason, they are bound to be fulfilled in their work and stay with the association as long as possible.

Norms: By pronouncing the association's objectives and plans for improvement, an authoritative mission can make guidelines to which its individuals can try to meet.

Representatives can find out if their activities and result line up with the qualities expressed in the mission

Instructions to Make an Authoritative Mission

Albeit a mission ought to be exceptional to the association that makes it, there are sure parts that a fruitful hierarchical mission ought to incorporate, like the association's motivation, values and objectives. You can follow these moves toward compose your very own authoritative mission:

1. Decide your motivation

Design is the explanation that an association exists. Numerous organizations fill comparative general needs, so it's vital to be basically as unambiguous as conceivable while pronouncing your association's motivation. For instance, an espresso organization's broadly useful is to sell espresso, yet its particular reason as it connects with its main goal ought to recognize it from contenders, for example, cultivating an appreciation for espresso and individuals who develop them.

2. Grasp your motivation

Realizing the thinking behind your motivation can assist you with composing an unmistakable, concise mission, and remembering the thinking for the discharge can convince partners to help your objective and your business. In the above illustration of the espresso organization, the originators could wish to feature the difficult work that goes into making espresso and to add to the ordinary bliss of individuals from the local area.

3. Decide your arrangement

Your arrangement alludes to how you expect to satisfy your motivation and the drawn out objectives that line up with it. This can be an overall proclamation of what the association does corresponding to its qualities. The espresso organization could express that it desires to achieve its objectives by selling top notch fair-exchange espresso at sensible costs to its clients.

The arrangement of selling "top notch fair-exchange espresso at sensible costs to its clients" characterizes the organization's goals, which illuminates its everyday tasks and can work as a blueprint for future business advancements.

4. Gather your main goal

Hierarchical missions are ordinarily a couple of sentences, and some are just an expression, so a great deal of data should fit in a little bundle. Give composing a shot a more drawn out form of your main goal that integrates your motivation, thinking and plan. Then see where you can eliminate words and join sentences to create the most brief assertion you can accomplish.

Instances of Hierarchical Missions

Seeing instances of hierarchical missions can provide you with a thought of how to think of one yourself.

Think about these instances of hierarchical missions, noticing the shifting lengths and arrangements:

Model 1

Organization: A café

Reason: Serving delectable home-style dinners in a family-accommodating climate

Plan: Giving enormous parts and an inviting encounter

Hierarchical Mission: "To give you an encounter that leaves your tummy and heart full."

This eatery's authoritative mission recommends that feasting with them is both actually fulfilling and sincerely charming.

Model 2

Organization: A business application designer

Reason: Further developing working environment correspondence

Plan: Giving a configuration that is alluring, simple to utilize and smoothed out

Hierarchical Mission: "Devoted to making a stage that addresses you and for you."

This model utilizes unique language that plays off the idea of correspondence to suggest that the engineer means to create applications that the two requests to clients and improves on working environment correspondence.

Model 3

Organization: An outerwear organization

Reason: Making solid, agreeable outerwear for all*

Plan: Giving a coat to foundation for each coat bought*

Hierarchical Mission: "With each acquisition of our outerwear, we give a comfortable coat to individual people in need."*

Here, the hierarchical mission straightforwardly states how the organization works and furthermore communicates its benefit of giving vital things to individuals who need them.

This cause's main goal includes the desire of its motivation and furthermore hoists it to be a much bigger thought. It supports the significance of the association's central goal.

This hierarchical mission conveys that the organization believes its clients should be satisfied with their experience.

If it's not too much trouble, note that none of the organizations referenced in this article are partnered with To be sure.

CHAPTER 2

WHY OBJECTIVE SETTING IS SIGNIFICANT?

Objectives are a significant piece of maintaining an effective business. They can give you a reasonable concentration, spur representatives and set focuses for your business to pursue.

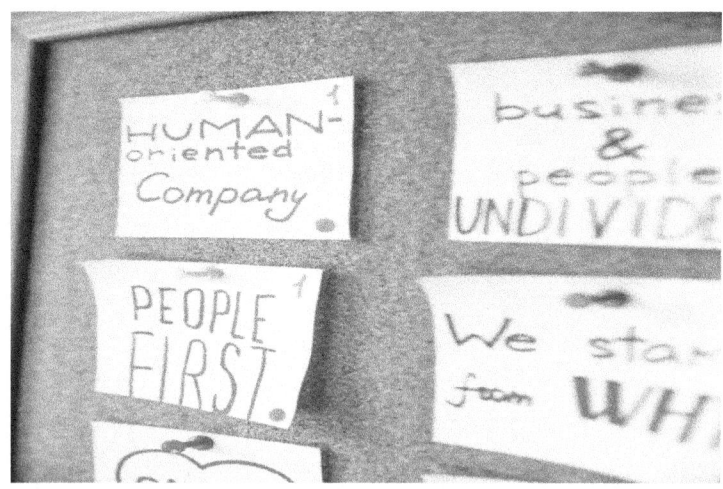

Objective setting can likewise give you a bunch of rules to check whether your business is succeeding. Having clear, obvious objectives can assist you with assuming command over your business' bearing and increment the possibilities accomplishing your bigger business targets.

Defining Brilliant objectives

Setting explicit, quantifiable, attainable, applicable and time bound objectives can assist you with centering your endeavors and increment the opportunity to effectively finish them. These viewpoints are vital to consider while making your objectives.

Illustration of a Savvy objective

How might explicit objectives have an effect? Think about this illustration of a dubious objective, and how this equivalent objective could be communicated in the wake of utilizing the Shrewd Technique:

Ambiguous objective: I need to assist my specialization with remaining on financial plan this year.

Brilliant objective: Every month, I will disseminate a spending plan report that shows our specialization's ongoing costs in contrast with our designated yearly spending plan and I will feature regions where we are overspending. In light of our ongoing spending, I will give thoughts on the most proficient method to cut expenses so we are back inside our financial plan.

Your Shrewd objective is presently something quantifiable and significant with enough particulars to assist you with accomplishing genuine outcomes. Continue to pursue to see precisely the way that we went from an unclear objective to a Brilliant objective.

We should investigate the five parts of making a Brilliant objective.

1. Make your objective Explicit

The most important phase in making a Shrewd objective is to make it explicit. Think about your objective in quantifiable terms by posing yourself the accompanying inquiries:

- What is it that I need to achieve?
- Will accomplishing this objective have a significant effect?
- What moves will I really want to make?

Applying Shrewd "Explicit" standards: "I will disperse a spending plan report."

2. Make your objective Quantifiable

This move toward the Savvy cycle prompts you to apply strategies for estimating your advancement toward accomplishing your objective. Being quantifiable additionally takes into account any moves you would execute to assist you with promoting your advancement toward your objective. For example, this might appear as following the time it makes you finish a move or meet an achievement.

Applying Brilliant "Quantifiable" models: "I will convey a financial plan report that shows our specialty's ongoing costs in contrast with our dispensed yearly spending plan."

3. Make your objective Attainable

This part of the Savvy technique connects with your objective being reachable. Do you have the assets and time expected to accomplish the objective? This might incorporate social occasion essential information, asking colleagues for help and mastering new abilities. You're bound to find success in your objective once it is explicit, quantifiable and considered reachable.

Applying Shrewd "Reachable" rules: "I will disperse a spending plan report that shows our specialty's ongoing costs in contrast with our designated yearly spending plan and I will feature regions where we are overspending."

4. Make your objective Pertinent

A significant objective will straightforwardly add to victories. Remember that each activity you take ought to draw you nearer to your objective. In our model, a significant objective will straightforwardly decrease costs.

Applying Savvy "Significant" measures: "I will disseminate a spending plan report that shows our specialty's ongoing costs in contrast with our designated yearly financial plan and I will feature regions where we are overspending. In view of our ongoing spending, I will give thoughts on the most proficient method to cut expenses so we are back inside our financial plan."

5. Make your objective Time sensitive

A time sensitive objective makes some particular memories cutoff time. You'll need to decide whether your objective is a present moment or long haul objective (or a blend of both). From that point, you can decide a course of events and set a timetable to comply with time constraints and achieve your goal. Your course of events ought to likewise be reasonable and permit you a lot of chances to make acclimations to your objective in regards to its significance, explicitness and reachability. Think about the last move toward the Savvy cycle in the accompanying model.

Applying Brilliant "Time sensitive" models: "Every month in the current year, I will circulate a spending plan report that shows our specialty's ongoing costs in contrast with our distributed yearly spending plan and I will feature regions where we are overspending. In light of our ongoing spending, I will give thoughts on the most proficient method to cut expenses so we are back inside our financial plan."

This objective presently fits every one of the models of a Savvy objective since it shows how explicit the goal is, frames a method for estimating progress, is reachable and pertinent to the ideal result, and sets up a timetable for every achievement.

Shrewd objectives can be a productive and significant instrument for groups while working together on projects.

Accomplishing Your Objectives

Whenever you have your rundown of business objectives, you'll have to get to work accomplishing them. Here are an interesting points while arranging your procedure to accomplish your business objectives:

Moves: Portray the singular activities you will make to pursue your objective. For instance, research five different frozen yogurt providers in Hobart and make a rundown of their upsides and downsides.

Time span: Set a cutoff time for finishing your objective. Ask yourself what amount of time you anticipate that the undertaking should require and set a reasonable date to pursue.

Assets: Detail your financial plan, staffing necessities and any provisions you'll have to achieve the objective.

Responsibility: Tell your staff, clients or a gathering you trust about your objectives. These individuals can assist you with keeping focused and ensure you are pursuing your objective.

Audit: Consider how you will quantify the outcome of your objective. Put time to the side to routinely audit how you are following towards it. Consider what moves you can make in the event that you are not on target.

Find What You Truly Care about

1. Self-Reflection

Journaling: Keep a diary to record your contemplations, dreams, and encounters. This training can assist you with revealing examples and wants.

Reflection: Invest energy in contemplation to clear your brain and spotlight on your internal identity. This can assist you with associating with your actual longings without outer interruptions.

Life Appraisal: Assess various parts of your life like profession, connections, wellbeing, and self-awareness. Distinguish where you feel satisfied and where you sense a need.

2. Distinguish Your Assets

Qualities Evaluation: Take a qualities evaluation test like the CliftonStrengths to acquire knowledge into your regular gifts.

Criticism from Others: Ask companions, family, and associates for their point of view on your assets. Now and again others can see qualities you could disregard.

Audit Past Triumphs: Think about past accomplishments and examine what abilities or characteristics added to your prosperity.

3. Picture Your Optimal Future

Vision Board: Make a dream board with pictures and words that address your objectives and goals. This visual portrayal can act as a day to day wake up call of what you're pursuing.

Future Self Activity: Compose a letter from your future self, portraying what you've accomplished and how you feel. This can assist you with explaining what you need to achieve.

Mind Planning: Utilize a psyche guide to investigate various parts of your optimal future. This can assist you with seeing associations and focus on your objectives.

4. Put forth Savvy Objectives

Explicit: Obviously characterize what you need to accomplish. Keep away from dubious objectives like "find success" and hold back nothing like "begin an effective web-based business."

Quantifiable: Lay out standards for estimating progress. This could be quantitative (e.g., income objectives) or subjective (e.g., consumer loyalty).

Reachable: Put forth sensible objectives that challenge you yet are feasible with exertion and assets.

Important: Guarantee your objectives line up with your more extensive life desires and values.

Time-bound: Set cutoff times to make a need to get going and assist you with remaining focused.

5. Separate key objectives.

Activity Plan: Make a step-by-step plan to achieve your goal. List all of the tasks you want to perform and focus on them.

Achievements: Set interim goals to track your progress and celebrate little triumphs along the way.

Using Time Productively: Schedule time to work on your goals. Predictable effort is essential for gaining progress.

6. Define Criticism and Mentorship: Find a tutor who can offer direction and assistance. Their experience can provide useful information and support.

Peer Support: Create a group or local area with similar objectives. Sharing experiences and hardships can inspire and bring new views.

Helpful Analysis: Be open to constructive feedback and utilize it to enhance your methods. Input may reveal opportunities for progress that you had not previously explored.

7. Remain adaptive.
Flexibility: Be prepared to adjust your goals when circumstances change. Life is unpredictable, thus adaptability is essential for long-term success.
Learning Outlook: Adopt a mindset of continuous learning. New information and experiences might help you establish and refine your goals.
Reconsideration: Periodically reassess your goals to ensure they are in line with your abilities and desires. It

is allowed to turn in the event that your requirements change.

8. Concentrate on your objectives.

Inspiration: Figure out what motivates you and use that to fuel your obligations. This could be a personal passion, a financial incentive, or a desire to assist others.

Discipline: Develop habits and schedules that help you achieve your goals. In any event, as motivation wanes, persistent effort is required for success.

Responsibility: Discuss your goals with someone who can hold you accountable. Standard registrations can help you keep on track and on schedule.

9. Recognize victories

Reward system: Establish an award system to acknowledge successes. This can help generate ideas and make the cycle more enticing.

Consider Your accomplishments: Take advantage of every opportunity to reflect on your accomplishments and growth. This can raise your confidence and make you more responsible.

10. Overcome Obstacles

Critical thinking: Improve your critical thinking skills to deal with challenges that arise. Maintain a positive mindset and seek clever answers.

Flexibility: Increase your adaptability by learning from setbacks and persevering through difficulties. Each impediment is a potential development opportunity.

Encourage a group of individuals. Count on your supportive community of people for support and assistance. Having individuals who believe in you can have a significant impact.

By deeply captivating in these ways, you can uncover what you genuinely need and set essential, attainable objectives that align with your guiding principles and desires.

Path to Prosperity
50

CHAPTER 3

MARGIN THE VISION, MISSION AND OBJECTIVES

Changing the vision, purpose, and objectives is essential for attaining long-term and focused growth in any business or unique goal. Here is a full advice on the best way to change these critical components:

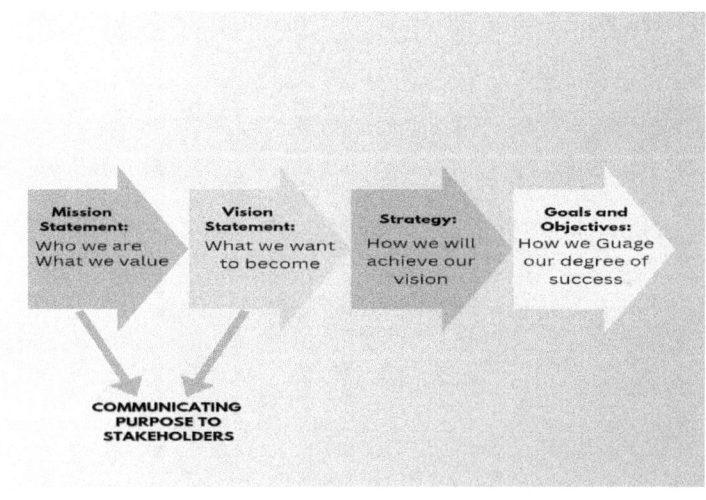

Definition: A vision is an optimistic declaration about what you want to accomplish in the long run. It is a forward-thinking declaration of where you or your business intend to go in the future.

Reason: The vision provides direction and motivation. It should be aggressive and compelling, acting as a guiding star for all subsequent planning and navigation.

Models:

Every individual's objective: "To carry on with a fair, sound, and satisfying life encompassed by friends and family."

A hierarchy of goals: "To be the leading provider of cost-effective energy arrangements around the world."

A mission statement defines the purpose of an organization or individual. It shows what you do, who you serve, and how you get things done.

Reason: The mission is more concrete and activity-oriented than the vision. It directs day-to-day operations and crucial initiatives, ensuring that everything done is consistent with the broader vision.

Models:

A goal of my own: "To help other people accomplish their wellness objectives through customized training and reasonable way of life changes."

The official mission is as follows: "To advance and convey maintainable energy arrangements that engage networks and safeguard the planet."

Objectives are clear, quantifiable, achievable, important, and time-bound goals that contribute to achieving the mission and vision.

Reason: Objectives specify certain milestones and stages. They divide a major mission into smaller, more achievable ones.

Models:

Individual objectives are as per the following: "Complete a critical distance race in less than 4 hours toward the following year's end."

Different scaled targets: "Increment maintainable power age by 20% inside the following five years."

Underestimating Vision, Mission, and Objectives

1. Portray your vision.

Lucidity: Guarantee that your vision is clear and compact. It ought to be not difficult to review.

Motivation: Make it animating and powerful to inspire enthusiasm and commitment.

2. Foster your central goal.

Congruity: Guarantee that the mission straightforwardly upholds the vision. It ought to decide how you will accomplish the vision.

The activity has been coordinated. Utilize dynamic language that plainly portrays what you do and how you get it moving.

3. Put forth Amazing Objectives

Express: Depict clear and cautious targets.

Quantifiable: Lay out standards to follow improvement and evaluate achievement.

Conceivable: Put forth fair and achievable objectives.

Proper: Guarantee that every objective lines up with the mission and adds to the vision.

Time-bound: Set cutoff times to increment decisive reasoning and consideration.

4. Guarantee consistency.

Consistency Check: Look at your targets consistently to guarantee that they reliably supplement your essential objective and vision.

Input Circle: Spread out an examination circle to assemble input from assistants and change contingent upon the situation.

5. Give Inner Correspondence: Guarantee all individuals from the association grasp the vision, mission, and objectives.

Outside Correspondence: Obviously convey your vision, goal, and objectives to accomplices, clients, and people overall.

6. Screen and Change Progress. Follow-up: Screen progress toward focus consistently. Utilize key execution pointers (KPIs) to evaluate achievement.

Adaptability: change points, methodologies, or even the mission if important to keep up with arrangement with the vision.

7. Perceive accomplishments.

Certification: Perceive and praise victories and wins. This causes everybody to feel improved and cultivates commitment to the vision and mission.

Reflection: Consider what worked best and what might be gotten to the next level. Utilize these encounters to work on future goals and methodology.

Blueprint Affiliation:

1. Depict Vision: Guarantee the drawn out objective is clear and enticing.

2. Develop Mission: Craftsmanship is a mission that moves toward the most common way of dealing with the vision.

3. Lay out Sagacious Targets: Depict clear, quantifiable, and time-bound objectives that help the mission.

4. Check for Consistency: Survey focuses consistently to guarantee that the technique lines up with the mission and vision.

5. Give Obviously: Guarantee that all accomplices and accessories get it and are centered around the vision, mission, and objectives.

6. Screen and Change: Screen progress, assemble examination, and be versatile in altering systems in view of the circumstance.

7. Perceive Accomplishments: Monitor your victories to remain roused and responsible.

By deliberately changing your vision, mission, and objectives, you make a strong and fundamental street to progression. This procedure guarantees that your endeavors and assets are all coordinated toward arriving at your definitive objectives.

Conquering Difficulties

Generally, all affiliations share the experience of experiencing boundaries. What recognizes one business from another, nonetheless, is the way they defeat business hindrances. While some permit snags to crash them, others have conceived techniques to get ready for themselves and accept they are a fabulous chance to learn and create.

A couple of obstructions can be kept away from. They may be the consequence of bungled feelings, unavoidable inclinations, and raising misconceptions. Unattended, these obstructions become affectionate criminals that take the local area, sap mental energy, and at times disturb the center longings.

How could you conquer these business leaps so you can hold onto significant possibilities for progress? Following are eight rules that might help you beat normal business issues.

Pay attention to your stomach with regards to individuals.

We as a whole have an implicit radar that lets us know when we are going to commit an error affecting individuals. However, we frequently decide not to regard that sign.

One of the reasons for startup disappointments is neglecting to employ skilled individuals to construct a compelling group. Picking the right group, particularly the right fellow benefactor, is critical. A few business visionaries pick a prime supporter in view of companionship — having been similar pals cooperating before. In the energy of beginning another endeavor, a business visionary might disregard the really strong inclination that lets them know the individual they are going to pick doesn't have the administrative ability for this job. They might need execution abilities or be frail in essential reasoning. Rather than supporting shortcomings, they compound them.

Recall that business ought not be private. For instance, in the event that you enlist a companion who ends up failing to meet expectations, it might very well be trying to settle on a convenient choice to let them go. Nonetheless, relentlessly failing to meet expectations, representatives will keep on hauling a business down. Thus, it is vital to have that troublesome discussion rapidly to bring about some benefit for the business.

Make Moderation an Organization Esteem.

It's normal to observe a startup that gets some financing and starts to spend like a Fortune 500 organization. Elation and the excitement of success can supplant good judgment. Uncontrolled spending is a business hindrance that can undoubtedly be stayed away from. In the beginning of Microsoft, they gave a "Shrimp and Weenies" reminder to all workers requesting that they be economical with organization cash — to arrange weenies, for instance, not shrimp, when the organization covers the bill. It requested that workers think about Microsoft "the greatest little organization on the planet." As your organization develops, saving an economical mindset is a word of wisdom for the long stretch.

Know your worth and stay away from close to home estimating.

One of the business challenges entrepreneurs frequently face is laying out legitimate valuing methodologies for their items and administrations. Now and again, feelings direct the cost charged. For instance, anxiety toward losing the deal and charging pretty much nothing, which over the long run will ceaselessly bring down the net revenue. This can make inconceivable business challenges not too far off. Close to home evaluating can likewise result from a deep satisfaction — what one specialist called "the delight of the chase," getting the agreement no matter what and feeling great that you beat the opposition. On nearer examination, this is an empty success — cost with your head, not your heart. Know your expenses, hold your ear to the ground in regards to your opposition, and occasionally reexamine your costs.

In the event that you consistently neglect to find a positive solution to your recommendations, ask clients for criticism on your valuing. Many are glad to share, and this input can yield supportive data going ahead.

Leave What Doesn't Work.

A few items or administrations remembered for a business may never again work. We will quite often become hopelessly enamored with our own items and administrations and find it hard to let something go. Maybe we foster blinders that keep us from seeing what's obvious to pariahs however not to us. As Gary Hamel put it in "What Is Important At This point: How to Win in a Universe of Constant Change, Fierce Rivalry, and Relentless Development, "There's a straightforward yet frequently disregarded illustration. To support achievement, you must forsake things that are as of now not effective."

Assess what doesn't work and dare to leave it before it becomes one of your business challenges. The energy you will have left out of letting it go will build your fixation on what works, permitting you to apply the force of careful attention to the right objective.

Supplant Old Systems With New Ones

Some business challenges result from our instilled propensities — gripping to obsolete modes and approaches to carrying on with work since it's what we know best. For instance, depending on outbound advertising strategies disregarding the worth of inbound showcasing methodologies. Inbound advertising is the brainchild of HubSpot. It implies drawing in clients through different roads like websites, webcasts, recordings, virtual entertainment promoting, and numerous different types of content advertising. It's the forerunner of outbound showcasing, which incorporates methodologies, for example, cold pitching and direct email advertising.

Being willing to investigate new showcasing strategies you might presently can't seem to utilize can assist you with developing your business and stay serious. Embrace web-based entertainment, make important substance to share uninhibitedly on your site, and consider recruiting an expert to assist you with improving your site or even re-appropriate your independent venture showcasing program.

Know The Greatest Business Snag You Face.

In the event that you could kill one major snag in your business that could permit you to develop dramatically, what might it be?

Normal reactions have been finding and preparing the ideal individuals to develop the business and how to track down more straightforward admittance to capital. What might your response be? Acquiring lucidity is the most important move toward making a move toward keeping impediments from hindering your street to progress.

For instance:

- Do you have deficient IT that pumps the brakes?
- Are there failures in utilizing innovation and programming?
- Could it be said that you are understaffed?
- Are individuals befuddled about jobs and obligations?
- Is the dynamic interaction slow in light of the fact that all choices should go through you?

- Is a developing responsibility dialing back progress?

Try Not to Limit Any Association With The Deals Capability.

During the startup stage, business visionaries by and large go about as deals bosses. They know their item or administration best since they made it. As they develop and begin to enlist staff, a few organizers might eliminate themselves from the deals capability. They gradually distance themselves as they center around supporting, individuals, the board, and other functional issues. That turns into a significant business hindrance since deals can represent the moment of truth of a business.

Standard counsel generally given to business people is to try not to wear an excessive number of caps and not to continuously fuss over the business. While this is valid, with regards to deals, it's judicious to constantly keep deals in your fringe vision so you are not surprised and can change before business impediments and business challenges stack up.

Besides, don't allow a bustling timetable to keep you from preparing or fostering your outreach group. Outreach groups are basic for any organization that needs to develop and succeed. Concentrating intently on giving continuous preparation to your outreach group is fundamental.

Adhere To The Sewing.

Streamline and remain fixed on what you know and what you excel at. All in all, adhere to the weaving. Tom Peters and Robert Waterman begat this saying in their fundamental book, Looking for Greatness: Examples From America's Best Run Organizations. As the creators put it some time in the past, be careful about business variety.

As the frequently rehashed aphorism goes: "New organizations pass on from acid reflux (taking on such a large number of things), not starvation (absence of chances)."

Inquiries to consider to try not to go off track in your business:

- What is central to the progress of your business?
- Which parts of your business are your bread and spread? That is, where does your association's essential pay come from? Where is the cash made?
- Who are your meat and potatoes clients?

Keep fixed on your center item or administration. Try not to layer more onto your business. In the event that you trust in your contribution and realize it adds esteem, it may not pay to search for the following energizing thing. Exhausting pays.

The Focus Points

Each business has difficulties. Knowing probably the most widely recognized business impediments and how to conquer them can set you and your business on a way for progress.

Estimating Your Advancement

Long haul business achievement doesn't simply result from compelling technique execution; it likewise depends on a comprehensive way to deal with observing, estimating, and assessing execution. This includes making unbiased and emotional measures — frequently called key Performance Indicators (KPIs).

Knowing how the various regions of your business are performing can assist you with surveying where your business is solid, where it is more vulnerable and factors you can improve. This ought to assist you with dealing with your exhibition proactively and proficiently.

You ought to gauge non-monetary focuses as well as thinking about monetary ones. Some others regions you could consider are:

Your Clients: e.g the number of you have, how frequently they use you and the number of clients you that have lost or acquired

Client support: e.g hanging tight times for help, objections, or reasons clients have grumbled.

piece of the pie - eg whether your portion of the market expanded or diminished against contenders

Your Staff: e.g fulfillment levels, work quality or participation records

Estimating Your Monetary Presentation

Your business achievement can rely upon creating and carrying out sound monetary and the executives frameworks. Numerous organizations fizzle as a result of poor monetary administration or arranging.

A survey of your monetary exhibition can assist you with reevaluating your business objectives and plan successfully for working on the business. While directing a monetary survey of your business, you should think about the accompanying:

Capital: This is the equilibrium of all of the cash streaming all through your business. You ought to guarantee that your estimate is routinely audited and refreshed.

Working Capital: Have your necessities changed? Assuming this is the case, research the explanations behind this development and evaluate how this thinks about the business standard. In the event that is essential, do whatever it may take to source extra capital.

Cost Base: Hold your costs under steady audit. Ensure that your expenses are shrouded in your deal cost - yet don't anticipate that your clients should pay for any business failures.

Acquiring: What is the place of any overdrafts or advances? Are there additional suitable or less expensive types of money you could utilize?

Development: Do you have plans set up to adjust your funding to oblige your business' changing requirements and development?

Estimating Your Productivity

One of the main regions of your funds you ought to audit is your productivity. Most developing organizations at last objective expanded benefits, so it means a lot to know how to quantify productivity. The key standard measures are:

Net revenue: How much cash is made after direct expenses of deals have been considered, or the commitment as it is likewise known.

Working Edge: This lies between the net and net proportions of benefit. Overheads are considered, yet interest and duty installments are not. Consequently, it is otherwise called the EBIT (profit before interest and duties) edge.

Net revenue: This is a much smaller proportion of benefits, as it considers all expenses, not simply direct ones. All overheads, as well as interest and expense installments, are remembered for the benefit computation.

Return on Capital Utilized: This works out net benefit as a level of the all out capital utilized in a business. This permits you to perceive how well the cash put resources into your business is performing contrasted and different ventures you could make with it, such as placing it in the bank.

Other Key Bookkeeping Proportions

There are various other generally utilized bookkeeping proportions that give helpful proportions of business execution. These include:

liquidity proportions, which inform you regarding your capacity to meet your transient monetary commitments

Productivity proportions, which let you know how well you are utilizing your business resources

Monetary influence or equipping proportions, which let you know how feasible your openness to long haul obligation is:

Returning to Your Business sectors

An essential business survey offers you the potential for success to have back from the action illustrated in your arrangement and take a gander at variables, for example,

- Changes in your market
- New and arising administrations
- Changes in your clients' necessities
- Outer factors like the economy, imports and new innovation
- Changes in cutthroat movement
- Taking a gander at your business according to your clients' point of view can assist you with trying not to get derailed when you think about your choices for development.

Client Criticism is Fundamental: the more you are familiar with what your clients think and need, the simpler it will be to deal with expanded quantities of clients. Search for however many approaches to catching this data as could reasonably be expected, including:

Deals Information: what your clients decide to purchase (or not to purchase) gives the most clear sign of their inclinations

Protests: however recollect that numerous clients will just switch providers prior to submitting a question

Surveys and Remark Cards: an extremely helpful wellspring of data, so consider utilizing motivators to urge more clients to finish them

Secret Shopping: having somebody act like a client for research purposes can give an exceptionally clear feeling of how well you are performing

Online Entertainment: this is a valuable approach to acquiring clients' criticism. In any case, in the event that you get negative criticism from a client, it can help you out on the off chance that you manage the client's remarks. It shows that you care about your clients.

Asking clients for input assists with distinguishing where upgrades can be made to your items or administrations, your staffing levels or your business methods

Augment Your Focus Beyond Current Clients

Offering more to existing clients may be the least demanding approach to expanding deals, yet most organizations holding back nothing should track down approaches to arriving at new gatherings of clients.

Partner With The Ideal Public

Your viewpoint on life, your gauge of yourself, your gauge of your worth are to a great extent shaded by your current circumstance. Your entire vocation will be changed, formed, shaped by your environmental elements, by the personality of individuals with whom you come in contact consistently.

Everything throughout everyday life and business is connected. All that you achieve or neglect to achieve will be bound up with others here and there. Your capacity to shape the right associations with the ideal individuals at each phase of your life and profession will be the basic determinant of your prosperity and accomplishment and will exorbitantly affect how rapidly you accomplish your objectives.

The more individuals you know, and who know you in a positive way, the more fruitful you will be at anything you endeavor. One individual, with flawless timing, perfectly positioned, can open an entryway for you that can completely change you and save you long periods of difficult work.

Nobody Does It Single-handedly

A vital piece of objective setting is for you to recognize individuals, gatherings and associations whose assistance you are willing to expect to accomplish your objectives. To achieve objectives of any sort, you will require the assistance of lots of individuals. Who are they?

There are three general classes of individuals whose assistance and participation you will expect in the years to come. These are individuals in and around your business, your loved ones, and individuals in gatherings and associations outside your business or group of friends. You really want to foster a technique to work successfully with each gathering.

Your Key Business Connections

Begin with your business. Who are the main individuals in your business life? What is your arrangement to foster greater associations with them? Make a rundown of each and every individual who works inside and beyond your business - your boss, partners, colleagues, subordinates, and particularly, your clients, suppliers and sellers. Which of these individuals have the more noteworthy capacity to help you or hurt you in the accomplishment of your business or vocation objectives?

Now and again, I request my crowds. What number of individuals present are in client assistance? A couple of hands go up. I then, at that point, bring up that everybody is occupied with client care, regardless of what they call it or what they do.

Distinguish Your Clients

A client can be characterized as anybody who you rely on for progress and headway in your work or business. A client can likewise be characterized as any individual who relies upon you in any capacity. By this set of definitions, nearly everybody around you is a client here and there.

For instance, your manager is your essential client at work. Your capacity to fulfill your manager will affect your future, your pay, and your vocation more than some other single ability you have. In the event that you disappoint every other person however your supervisor is happy with you, you will have no problem at all in your work. If it's all the same to everybody inside and outside your organization yet your supervisor is discontent with you, that issue alone can cut off the future.

Your Client support Procedure

One of the best-systems you can utilize is to make a rundown of all that you accept that you have been employed to do. Answer the inquiry, "For what reason am I in finance?" And record all that you can imagine. Then, at that point, take this rundown to your chief and request that your manager coordinate this rundown arranged by their need. What means a lot to your chief? What is second generally significant? What is generally significant? Etc.

Two Vital Characteristics for Promotability

In a Survey Reported in Progress Magazine, a couple of years prior, 104 CEOs were given twenty characteristics of an optimal representative and requested to choose the most significant. Eight-six percent of the senior leaders chose two characteristics as being more significant for profession achievement and headway than some other. First was the capacity to define boundaries; to isolate the important from the superfluous. Second was the capacity to take care of business quickly; to rapidly execute.

Nothing will help you more in your profession than to get the standing for being the sort of individual who finishes the main occupation rapidly and well.

Difficult Work on Some Unacceptable Assignment?

Be that as it may, here's the trick. Many individuals are taking a stab at their positions, yet they are not dealing with what their supervisor views as the main work. That's what the miserable truth is assuming you make an irrelevant showing well overall, this could hurt your vocation and even compromise your work.

As conditions change, keep the lines of correspondence open with your chief. Be certain that what you are doing is as yet your manager's first concern. And afterward make a round of doing it quick. Nothing makes a manager more joyful than having somebody who takes care of business rapidly. Be certain that you are that individual.

Your Other Key Clients

Your colleagues, who additionally rely upon your work, are your clients too. Go to every last one of them and inquire as to whether there is anything that you can do to help them. Inquire as to whether there is whatever that you might accomplish a greater amount of or less of, whatever that you might begin or quit doing that would assist them with taking care of their responsibilities better.

The truth of the matter is that individuals ponder themselves and their own dandies the entire day. Whenever you propose to assist people to go about their responsibilities better or quicker, they will be completely open to aiding you later. The Law of Planting and Procuring isn't the Law of Harvesting and Planting. There is a specific request to this regulation. First you put in, and afterward you get out. First you sow, and afterward you procure.

You ought to search for a valuable open door in your work to help individuals and to do decent things for other people. Each fair effort you get back in the saddle to you somehow or another, sooner or later, and frequently out of nowhere. The most well known individuals in each association are the people who are continuously ready to loan some assistance.

The more individuals close to you, above you, and underneath you like you and backing you, the more you will get compensated and the quicker you will advance. Foster stands as a "go-provider," as well, similar to a hard worker.

Search for ways of being an important asset to individuals around you and they will consequently search for approaches to help you and support you when you most need it.

Deal with Your Time Well
What is using time productively?

Using time effectively includes arranging how to proficiently utilize and intentionally control the time you spend to amplify efficiency. So, time usage assists you with accomplishing more quicker than expected. Different potential gains include:

- Better work quality
- Less pressure
- Additional opportunity to chip away at vital or inventive undertakings
- Less lingering
- More self-assurance

Why is Using Time Productively Significant?

A powerful time usage procedure can make your business day more proficient and viable. Look at these time usage tips to assist with changing your work.

Comply with Your Time constraints: Deal with your time, and it'll be simpler to convey your work on time. With the right systems, you can abandon the times of stalling and last-minute packing before cutoff times.

At any point focus on Your Errands: Do you take a gander at your plan for the day and not know where to begin? Using time productively can assist you with focusing on better so you burn through less time concluding which assignments to handle first.

Make heads or tails of Your Responsibility. In the event that you're feeling overpowered by how much work on your plate, tracking down a more powerful method for dealing with your time can make it simpler to shuffle your errands.

Enjoy More Reprieves: Execute a superior time usage methodology so you can tick off your morning to-do things by noon and can quit managing your lunch break.

Make Additional Opportunity for Yourself: Do you frequently find your average business day seeping into off-work hours? Solid using time effectively can assist you with containing business related errands to your everyday job, giving you additional opportunity for yourself.

Master Exhortation On the most proficient method to All the more likely Deal with Your Time

This is the way to get everything rolling, planning a superior time usage schedule.

1. Realize how you're investing your energy

On the off chance that your efficiency is estimated by yield over a specific period, lost time can mean dollars through the window. Very much like making a financial plan, you need to follow what you're really investing your energy into to uncover any regions or propensities that are hindering you from arriving at your objectives.

Begin with a period check. Time-following devices, for example, Gather and TrackingTime can coordinate straightforwardly into your Leeway work area, and they can perceive you, in view of the classes you set up, how long you're useful in a day versus how long you're spending on non-business related exercises, like perusing virtual entertainment or shopping.

2. Adhere to an everyday timetable

Go past "I have eight hours to do XYZ." Make an everyday timetable with distributed time blocks for various errands. Adhering to it is the way to progress.

Make reasonable timetables. Individuals misjudge their ability to finish things, a peculiarity researchers call "arranging paradox," which as a rule brings about excessively hopeful conveyance gauges. Add time cushions between assignments so that regardless of whether one goes throughout as far as possible, the general timetable stays in one piece.

Really focus: Try not to sneak to non-business related destinations (or anything it is you shouldn't do) during work hours. Close every one of those "for some other time" program tabs. Switch off your telephone or stash it far off until it's the ideal opportunity for a planned break. Once more, self-control is your dearest companion here

3. Focus on

Daily agendas can be efficiency lifelines. Yet, if you don't watch out, they can get so enormous and overpowering that you don't have the foggiest idea where to begin. An instrument known as the Eisenhower Network can assist you with choosing what to focus on as per significance and desperation. Utilizing this choice lattice, you can separate your rundown by:

Do right away: Significant errands with characterized cutoff times, or ones you've procrastinated on for such a long time they're presently past due

Plan for some other time: Significant undertakings with no characterized cutoff times

Delegate: Errands that another person can do

Erase: Undertakings you can wipe out in light of the fact that they're not basic to your objectives or mission

4. Computerize Monotonous Assignments

Representatives who computerize are 71% bound to surpass supervisors' assumptions, as we learned in the Territory of Work report. At the point when you mechanize drawn-out or tedious work, it can save important time, permitting you to zero in on additional complicated and imaginative parts of your work.

With devices like Leeway's Work process Developer, you can make robotizations that are as basic or as perplexing as you'd like. They might be associated with the other applications and administrations you use to finish work. Furthermore, in light of the fact that no coding abilities are essential, anybody, no matter what their specialized foundation, can send mechanizations with only a couple of snaps.

5. Tackle the Most Troublesome Undertaking First

Interruptions happen to us all, whether it's a call, some help from a partner or that heap of filthy dishes. Before you know it, the day is no more.

The Eat That Frog efficiency technique concocted by authority master Brian Tracy functions admirably for individuals who will quite often dawdle or experience difficulty keeping away from interruptions. It suggests handling the greatest, most troublesome and most significant undertaking first — the one you're probably going to procrastinate on for some other time. Just continue on toward different things once you've "eaten that frog."

Cluster Process Comparable Undertakings

Bunching, or cluster handling, implies gathering comparative errands so you can deal with them together. Bunch them by goal or capability.

For instance:

Client gatherings on Wednesdays and Thursdays
Answer messages from 10 a.m. to 11 a.m. as it were
Create reports first thing, and disperse

6. Set man-made intelligence to Work for Search and Synopses

Envision having an associate that slices through the commotion, giving you simply the data you really want, when you want it. Man-made brainpower supports your efficiency by addressing your inquiries, summing up discussions and making content like attempts to sell something and blog frames. It assists you with finding pertinent data rapidly, centers around significant undertakings and deals with your time better so you can accomplish more.

7. Set sensible time limits

That's what parkinson's regulation expresses, "Work extends to occupy the time apportioned to finish it."

In the event that you have an entire day to follow through with two jobs that ought to require just three hours, you'll most likely still go through the entire day on those two undertakings. In the event that you give yourself a more modest window, odds are you'll in any case fulfill the previous time constraint.

8. Realize when to say no

We have just such a lot of energy in a day, and it disappears with the hours. To stay away from insane work, know your cutoff points and say no. Perceive your assets and shortcomings. Center around what you're great at and, if conceivable, delegate what should be possible better and quicker by others.

9. Keep away from performing various tasks

The science is sure about performing multiple tasks: It cuts proficiency and might actually be risky. As indicated by the American Mental Affiliation, mental shuffling includes "exchanging costs" that cut efficiency. Despite the fact that undertaking exchanging could cost a couple of moments for each switch, it adds up on the off chance that you perform multiple tasks much of the time. Your gamble for blunder likewise takes off.

10. Keep things coordinated

You could require an association makeover if any of these have happened to you:

Late to a gathering you're driving

Neglected to print out a report your manager required for a show

Needed to ask IT for your username or secret key at least a time or two

Fortunately association is an expertise that can be mastered. Begin with the rudiments.

Keep a spotless work area: Public Geographic reports that clinicians and neuroscientists connect the impacts of messiness on discernment, psychological wellness and conduct. Visual mess can increment feelings of anxiety and uneasiness, setting off a survival reaction. For better independent direction, throw any papers that can be destroyed or reused. Get out unnecessary items and put everyday devices inside simple reach.

Coordinate your PC documents and shared drives: Record naming is critical to arranging advanced documents. Make a framework that permits you and your partners to find things rapidly and without any problem.

Utilize a schedule: Coordinate your schedule by life containers, for example, "individual," "expert" and "responsibility." Attempt variety coding to rapidly separate classes or by earnest versus non-critical.

CHAPTER 4

MONETARY ADMINISTRATION FOR PROGRESS

For What Reason is Monetary Administration Significant?

Monetary administration empowers you to make achievements in day to day monetary targets. A decent framework will permit you to:

- Be proactive and not responsive to circumstances
- Acquire effectively depending on the situation by preparing
- Share financial plan data with your investor to improve on the advance endorsement process
- Update financial backers on monetary arranging data
- Have beneficial and productive activities
- Access a decent dynamic instrument while thinking about key monetary issues

On the miniature level, strong monetary preparation and control enables you by:

- Staying away from superfluous weighty interests in fixed resources

- Keeping up with an adequate number of momentary working capital requirements that help stock and records receivable assortments
- Defining deals objectives that are development situated and not just working as a request taker
- Further developing net revenues with compelling estimating of labor and products
- Decreasing direct work costs, provider costs and different things that influence the expense of merchandise sold
- Working proficiently with generally speaking authoritative costs
- Performing better expense arranging
- Playing out a responsiveness examination, which decides what free factors will mean for a choice

Preparing for worker benefits

Motivations to Foster a Monetary Administration Framework

The most important move towards fostering a decent monetary administration framework is to make budget summaries. Creating these assertions month to month permits you to oversee proactively for designated achievement. Significant budget summaries to keep up with incorporate a monetary record, income proclamation and pay explanation.

Fostering a monetary administration framework assists with overseeing capital uses that each business should consider. As a general rule, you make resource buys to produce pay. Any monetary contemplations connected with capital consumptions ought to be offset with the sum it takes to make the buy and the pay it will deliver. Dealing with your capital uses actually guarantees you won't overstretch the business by getting excessively. Pay produced ought to legitimize the cost.

One more motivation to foster a monetary administration framework is to deal with your income. Working costs, for example, finance, office supplies, protection and utilities should be paid. You need to look forward to perceive how much is expected in your records receivable and whether meeting those costs by the due dates is sufficient. Better administration of your income is conceivable assuming you abbreviate how much time clients need to pay solicitations. Furthermore, you could rework due dates with sellers.

One of the essential monetary obligations of any business is to keep costs as low as could really be expected. You can endeavor to achieve this in numerous ways like requesting that merchants lower costs, diminish staff or lessen energy use - all without compromising the nature of business creation. All things considered, on the off chance that you don't oversee costs, your business will be on an unending cycle to remain above water just to pay functional expenses.

Paying expenses is a sureness in your own life and business. You have a monetary obligation to anticipate installments to neighborhood and government burdening specialists. If not, benefits can vanish in punishments and interest on late installments. Charge arranging includes ensuring there is sufficient money close by to make assessed charge installments each quarter they come due. Neglecting to design and boost accessible derivations will cost more in duties and leave less to put resources into the development of your business.

Jobs inside a Monetary Administration Framework

There are a few significant jobs that a decent monetary administration framework has in the progress of your business. Thus, you ought to incorporate this framework as a critical part to by and large hierarchical administration. Vital and strategic objectives are remembered for monetary administration to guarantee monetary assets are utilized admirably and successfully. A portion of the particular jobs inside a monetary administration framework include:

- Bookkeeping and accounting
- Creditor liabilities and receivable
- Speculations and dangers
- Bookkeeping and Accounting

Regularly, a monetary administration framework will distinguish, record, measure and correspond monetary data about a business. The establishment for this framework is to have great accounting rehearses. Whether you recruit somebody in-house or utilize an external element, accounting gives precise and complete data to your bookkeeper to execute monetary assignments. Where bookkeeping manages the generally speaking monetary strength of your business, accounting handles explicit, everyday exchanges.

Creditor liabilities and Records Receivable

Creditor liabilities is answerable for data about your sellers and providers. This piece of the monetary framework shows how much things cost, how installments were made and some other insights concerning an exchange. There ought to likewise be a record of exceptional cash owed to merchants and providers. Likewise, creditor liabilities show the advancement of the work process, which permits you to endorse solicitations for installment.

Where creditor liabilities is answerable for cash outpourings, money due records cash inflows. The job of records receivable is to monitor what clients owe through solicitations and update warnings for any remaining installments. Money due assists your business with recuperating past due solicitations before they enter the awful obligation domain.

Ventures and Dangers

One more fundamental job for the monetary administration framework is to find amazing open doors that will benefit or supplement your business. The main way you can take advantage of speculative valuable open doors is to pay for the ideal acquisitions when they happen. While your group finds potential open doors, great monetary administration guarantees a proficient and viable cycle. Through various parts of your monetary framework, you can assess the business' general wellbeing for making such ventures.

In like manner, you need to have the option to assess gambles, whether with a speculation opportunity or different regions cautiously. This might incorporate recruiting more staff or making a capital buy. Assessment takes a gander at the ongoing business sector to decide whether it is the best chance to make such speculations.

Seeing dangers settles an essential objective of your monetary administration framework: limiting dangers with procedures that balance unanticipated liabilities. You need to have sufficient protection inclusion for workers, gear and property. Controlling obligation and having a powerful acknowledged framework for monetary establishments and providers gives your business more functional adaptability and less monetary gamble on the off chance that you experience income issues.

Monetary Administration is More Than Keeping Precise Records

Past keeping exact records and adjusting the organization checkbook, monetary administration is significant for your business achievement. You need a decent monetary framework that assists you with using wise judgment without overspending. It is critical to be ready for consumptions and benefit circulations. Poor monetary administration influences all regions of your business. Great monetary administration guarantees that what your business achieves everyday isn't lost on inefficient spending.

Fixing Your Business

Can we just be real for a moment: income is the soul that supports any business. Entrepreneurs generally expect clients or clients will pay on time yet when they don't, we would rather not cause trouble by requesting installment. Income of the executives is essential, yet whenever done ineffectively, numerous organizations might be confronted with shutting its entryways. In the event that an entrepreneur is exclusively centered around pursuing the following deal and not following the condition of current agreements, they can be caught unaware by deals that might be on the books however not in the bank.

1. Lay out More limited Assortment Period

There is an immediate relationship between how much a business can put resources into its own development and its DSO (Days Deals Remarkable), which is urgent to its capacity to remain in business and flourish against competition. In bookkeeping terms, the DSO is the time span it takes an organization to gather on solicitations. On the off chance that an organization takes too lengthy to even consider gathering on extraordinary solicitations, the income is affected in a bad way and organizations making due on sluggish income are dependent upon an unavoidable misfortune. Nonetheless, a short circle back on gathering receivables implies the organization will be situated to harvest benefits all the more promptly and yet again put those benefits in its proceeds with development.

2. Track Installments Effectively

Laying out brief timeframes to gather receivables is only the start of getting compensated, yet it's adequately not. Neither does it guarantee speedy, steady circle back on the receivables (installments), which is the reason the organization must proactively pursue its cash. Before this happens, recommend the organization protect against any unanticipated hiccups, for instance, by ensuring all solicitations are exact and conveyed on time. Verifying whether the installment terms and due dates are obviously imparted. If any of the organization's contact data (e.g., charging address, telephone number, resource, and so forth) has changed since the last charging, ensure the new data is reflected in the solicitations. Whenever you've hailed and prepared for possible mistakes on your end, start settling on decisions the second solicitations are sent.

3. Review Past due Record

Obviously, numerous installments aren't made by the mentioned due date. Subsequently, organizations should regularly follow every one of their records/agreements to guarantee installment for items or administrations given and to keep a constant flow of income to fuel and safeguard the lifesaver of the business. Routine reviews take out superfluous worry about gathering the "old and owed." Obviously, on-time paid solicitations are the assumption, however guess those times when you'll be tested in gathering from clients who will not pay, for whatever the explanation. There are a few reasonable advances you can take that might bring about installment, for example, talking genially to the party in question, diminishing what is owed, breaking the installment into sensible terms or offering numerous installment techniques.

4. Distinguish Littlest Records To Begin Assortment

Sort every one of your exceptional records from biggest to littlest. Begin with the littlest sums due and continue to gather monies owed. The upside of beginning with the littlest sums is that they might demonstrate the most un-challenging to recover or arrange. Abstaining from more modest records helps gather speed and certainty that the bigger records can be effectively gathered and additionally haggled too.

5. Issue Solicitations To Pay on Receipt

Structure your agreements and solicitations to be paid upon conveyance. Limit or consider disposing of the utilization of net 30 or 60-day installment terms, which may unintentionally empower late installments and unfavorably influence the organization's capacity to monetarily develop. Whenever an installment is made late, now is the ideal time to charge once more, and thus, another late installment is probably going to be submitted. This installment arrangement puts your business on a merry-go-round of being paid late over and over. Receipt clients promptly upon fruition of a help. Once more, follow up rapidly at whatever point installment is postponed. A records receivable report created naturally by the bookkeeping programming or group will show where those cash spills are. Depend on the report and use it for call planning and following. On the off chance that you (by and by) lack the opportunity to settle on these subsequent decisions, consider getting help, ideally one that can take installments via telephone and on the spot!

Supporting Your Triumph

Each organization needs to develop their business, yet hardly any skill to support it as long as possible or look past the following quarterly or yearly report. Growing a business requires the right scholarly capital, painstakingly chosen key associations, and items or potentially benefits areas of strength for with request. Past these essentials, supporting development requires serious areas of strength for an establishment - to lessen the dangers to the business after some time.

One of my clients has been doing business for over 15 years. They are an innovation organization with a solid incentive and administration offering. Yet, while the plan of action is versatile, it misses the mark of serious areas of strength from which to put resources into its development with certainty. The President realizes that business income can surpass its current base of $250 million (that is beneficial), yet there is an absence of top ability, conflicting functional efficiencies and generally speaking initiative that is reluctant to deal with development directly. This dials back development and makes it hard to reliably support clients, plan a work environment culture that can assist representatives with flourishing, form the right groups to build efficiency, and structure the outside associations to settle on the right essential choices to make a billion dollar association.

It could be said that being a $250 million business is sufficient and - for the previously mentioned reasons - it ought to be offered to an association that has the status to develop and support it, instead of putting away great cash without knowing the likelihood for ideal return for money invested.

Before your business can develop and support its energy, you should make a move on the side of the accompanying six things to guarantee your organization constructs major areas of strength for a for long haul achievement:

1. **Top Ability:**

Without the ideal individuals, a business can't develop and it positively makes it hard to support energy over the long run. Business is about individuals and without the ideal individuals a business can't develop and develop. As a rule, this requires an association to revive its ability pool on the side of the association's plan of action and the novel necessities of its clients.

Rethink your ability and pose yourself this inquiry: Is your ongoing ability pool overhauling your clients and distinguishing the ideal times to make and support business development? Is it safe to say that they are empowering their enthusiastic interests looking for vast potential outcomes in their work? Take this test and check whether your groups can successfully see, sow, develop and share open doors in their work. Assuming you score north of 35, you are looking great. If not, you have work to do.

2. **Functional Efficiencies**

Efficiencies drive costs down and implant a mentality inside the working environment culture that makes individuals delicate to expenses and ways of smoothing out how the association conveys, works and draws an obvious conclusion of chances. This assists with guaranteeing that exercises inside the association are in arrangement with the requirements of the business to make and support development.

The most ideal way to make functional efficiencies is to guarantee that the working environment culture upholds the devices to drive efficiencies inside the association - by plan - not unintentionally. To find out more, the following are six authoritative qualities to make and support development through an efficiencies-driven mentality. Eventually, your association should embrace a social commitment that stands by the accompanying saying: Achievement comes most to the individuals who are encircled by individuals who believe their prosperity should proceed.

3. Prospecting the Right Clients

Business person is presently not simply a business term any longer, it's a lifestyle. You should continuously embrace a pioneering mentality to see and immediately jump all over the right chances - particularly those beforehand inconspicuous or that others don't see by any means. For this reason you should embrace an innovative soul while prospecting the right clients - to guarantee the business develops, however supports itself over the long haul.

It is all comparative with Create deals. On the off chance that you are offering to clients whose business needs are not feasible - this addresses a lose situation. In the event that you don't have the right systems set up to prospect the right clients, you will find it challenging to support development - not to mention develop by any stretch of the imagination.

Embracing an enterprising demeanor permits you to see past the self-evident and spot the best clients on the side of your plan of action. This keeps securing costs low and guarantees client connections are commonly gainful and objectives are in arrangement.

4. Cool headed Direction

Critical thinking is the pith of what pioneers exist to do. As pioneers, our goal is to minimize the occurrence of problems, which means we must be bold enough to confront them directly. We should be strong in our mission to make and support energy for the association and individuals we serve.

At the point when an association has the conventions, the standard working systems set up to take care of issues and use wise judgment, they have empowered the capacity to expect the unforeseen to guarantee that conditions don't pressure them into action. It's hard to support development when you work in a climate where individuals are continually being excessively responsive, as opposed to proactive. Steady navigation involves great judgment and the capacity to recognize ideal timing and profundity - to guarantee that energy is made and never disturbed.

5. Incredible Administration

The best chiefs are instinctual leaders and in this manner have the round vision to see a valuable open door in all things. Having done it - decided - so often all through their vocations, incredible pioneers will become resistant to pressure circumstances and very natural about projecting key, long haul plans for what's in store.

Supporting business development requests authority that can consider the glass to be half full - in any event, when every other person is considering it to be half unfilled.

6. Go ahead and Develop

To support development, you should have the outlook of embracing risk as your dearest companion. The second that workers are not urged to share their thoughts and goals, it becomes hard to take responsibility for necessities of the business - and the commercial center rapidly starts to cruise you by.

Supporting development expects you to impart your force to other people. It requests that you have the wellbeing of others in your group, and partners all through the association, on the most fundamental level. Driving practical development can never happen alone. It requests areas of strength for a, however cooperative divisions/specialty units that together make up serious areas of strength for a with the right scholarly capital.

At the point when variety of belief is embraced, it fills in as a strong unifier to use one of a kind reasoning and the open doors related with it - to support development.

At the point when supportability turns out to be important for your authoritative focal ethos, you're not just better ready to support business development - you're ready to stay five strides on the ball. To arrive, pioneers should be strong trailblazers — blasting new ways few would see the entire way to completion, not to mention go down in any case. This can fuel valuable open doors beforehand and mix the working environment and representative commitment with freshly discovered reason and fervor - further supporting the development of the business.

CONCLUSION

ACHIEVING BUSINESS SUCCESS

Accomplishing business greatness includes reliably conveying excellent items or administrations, keeping up with effective tasks, and encouraging a culture of consistent improvement.

Here are key techniques to accomplish business greatness:

1. Initiative and Vision

Clear Vision and Mission: Characterize an unmistakable vision and mission that directs the association's essential course. Convey this vision to all workers to guarantee arrangement.

Successful Initiative: Pioneers ought to rouse and spur representatives, encouraging a positive and comprehensive workplace. They ought to show others how it's done and be focused on greatness.

2. Client Concentration

Understanding Client Needs: Consistently assemble and break down client criticism to grasp their requirements and assumptions.

Surpassing Assumptions: Plan to meet as well as surpass client assumptions by conveying unrivaled quality and administration.

3. Functional Greatness

Proficient Cycles: Carry out lean standards and consistent improvement strategies (like Six Sigma) to smooth out tasks, lessen squander, and further develop effectiveness.

Quality Administration: Lay out powerful quality administration frameworks (e.g., ISO 9001) to guarantee predictable item/administration quality.

4. innovation and Versatility

Empower Development: Cultivate a culture of advancement where representatives are urged to think of groundbreaking thoughts and arrangements.

Flexibility: Be coordinated and versatile to changing economic situations, mechanical headways, and client inclinations.

5. Representative Commitment and Advancement

Representative Preparation and Advancement: Put resources into worker preparing and proficient improvement to upgrade abilities and capabilities.

Commitment and Strengthening: Connect with workers in dynamic cycles and enable them to step up and obligation.

6. Execution Estimation

Key Execution Markers (KPIs): Characterize and routinely screen KPIs to quantify execution against vital objectives.

Benchmarking: Contrast execution and industry principles and best practices to distinguish regions for development.

7. Manageability and Corporate Obligation

Reasonable Practices: Incorporate maintainable practices into business activities to limit ecological effect and advance social obligation.

Corporate Social Obligation (CSR): Participate in CSR exercises that add to the prosperity of the local area and society

8. Innovation and Computerized Change

Influence Innovation: Use trend setting innovations (like artificial intelligence, enormous information, and robotization) to upgrade effectiveness, further develop independent direction, and convey better client encounters.

Advanced Change: Embrace computerized change to remain serious and applicable in the advanced age.

9. Vital Associations and Cooperation

Vital Unions: Structure key associations and collusions to use reciprocal qualities and abilities.

Joint effort: Cultivate a cooperative climate both inside the association and with outer partners.

Accomplishing business greatness is a continuous excursion that requires a comprehensive methodology,

incorporating initiative, client center, functional proficiency, development, representative commitment, execution estimation, manageability, innovation, and vital organizations. By sticking to these standards, organizations can accomplish supported development, benefit, and upper hand.

www.ingramcontent.com/pod-product-compliance
Lightning Source LLC
Chambersburg PA
CBHW050310230526
45471CB00005B/2105